THE HOLY GHOST

GOD'S GIFT OF POWER TO EVERY GROWING CHRISTIAN

SECOND EDITION

JOHN L. GODBOLT, Ph.D.

Copyright

DEDICATION

I dedicate this project to the memory of my late father, Roy L. Godbolt, a true servant leader in the home, church, and community.

ACKNOWLEDGEMENTS

When you assemble a team to discuss the Holy Ghost and Fire, they must be skilled and filled. This team knows their craft and they have the gift of the Holy Spirit living in theme. Thank you for the energy and effort you spent on this project. I am more grateful for you today than I was when we began.

To my proofreaders, Helenea Dawson and Delarese Townsend, you are an amazing gift to the Body of Christ. Thank you for your wise counsel. We could not have done this project without you.

A special thank you to April M. Collins for your time invested in the restructuring of this work; we appreciate you!

To my mother and father, Reatha and the late Roy Godbolt, your efforts to raise my siblings and me in an environment of love and respect has paid off. I love you!

To our family, Jocelyn and Terrence, Royvell and Crystal, Terrence (TJ), Jaymond, Iyanna, Jaelin, John Jr., and Christian, I am so proud of your commitment to be leaders and not followers.

And to my dear wife and friend, Vertell, it is still a joy to come home to your smile and entertaining voice. You add such light to my life. You are the reason this project is real and weighty with nuggets of wisdom. I love you!

CONTENTS

The Holy Ghost: Introduction

God's gift of power to every growing Christian!

Joel 2:28, 29 And it shall come to pass afterward, that I will pour out my spirit upon all flesh; and your sons and your daughters shall prophesy, your old men shall dream dreams, your young men shall see visions: And also upon the servants and upon the handmaids in those days will I pour out my spirit.

First and foremost, God made a promise to send us a gift that comforts and empowers us beyond our own natural ability. The Holy Ghost, also referred to as the Holy Spirit, is that gift. He not only gives us power to do great things outwardly, but the Holy Spirit also changes the inward man.

God gave us two natural signs that are counterparts to the Holy Ghost and Fire - the dove and natural fire. In this self-guided study, we will explore these natural signs to help us better understand how the Holy Spirit can work in our lives.

My hope is that you will be inspired to seek a more intimate relationship with Jesus which will cultivate a thirst for more of His guidance, wisdom, and understanding. The objective of this study is to discuss who The Holy Ghost is in the earth, how to receive Him, and what He empowers us to do.

The Author

How To:

Within this booklet you will find space provided for you to take notes and bible journal. Bible journaling is a unique way to engage with scripture. For each scripture, insert yourself into the necessary sections as well as crossing out words and inserting synonyms. This method can help you better understand scripture. Please see the example below:

King James Version:

1 Corinthians 12:7 | But the manifestation of the Spirit is given to every man to profit withal.

Bible Journaling

1 Corinthians 12:7 | But the demonstration of the Spirit is given to _____ to benefit also. (insert your name)

Here, you see where you can use other words to make the scripture more personable. Now it's time for you to try it!

Part One:
The Natural and Spiritual Transforming Power of Fire

Anything that a natural fire can do, the Holy Ghost Fire will do in the spirit realm because it is the spiritual side to natural fire. Our old man, known as the carnal nature, needs to be transformed by the Fire of the Holy Ghost. A natural fire can warm (comfort), cook (complete), light (enlighten) and burn up (consume). In our journey of growth and development in Christ Jesus, we need this gift operating in our lives so that any aspect of our life that is unlike Jesus can be conformed to the image of Christ.

> Acts 1:8 - *But ye shall receive power, after that the Holy Ghost is come upon you: and ye shall be witnesses unto me both in Jerusalem, and in all Judaea, and in Samaria, and unto the uttermost part of the earth.*

Journaling Moment: Write the above scripture in a way you can understand it:

_____

_____

_____

_____

Jesus spoke these words to those committed to carrying the gospel or good news to a dying world. Since we are called to share our testimony of salvation, healing, and deliverances with others, we need a power beyond our own energy and charisma. That is why Jesus said, I am sending the Holy Ghost and He will endow you with power.

Remember, everything that a natural fire can do, the power of the Holy Ghost does in the Spirit, either to and/or for us. So, what is this power?

1. **Fire lights the way** - Luke 12:12 - *"For the Holy Ghost shall teach you in the same hour what ye ought to say."*

   When we are endowed with the Holy Spirit, our minds receive the light of understanding. When we are lost and feel confused, the Holy Spirit gives understanding that lights our way.

2. **Fire comforts us** - John 14:26 - *"But the Comforter, which is the Holy Ghost, whom the Father will send in my name, he shall teach you all things, and bring all things to your remembrance, whatsoever I have said unto you."*

   A natural fire offers comfort. The crackling sound of a campfire and the happy chatter of family while enjoying a casual meal can bring a comfort that is not difficult to imagine. This is also the nature of the Holy Ghost. He will release His presence to comfort you when your faith is being tested by life's ups and downs.

3. **Fire consumes** - I Corinthians 6:19, 20 *"What? know ye not that your body is the temple of the Holy Ghost which is in you, which ye have of God, and ye are not your own? For ye are bought with a price: therefore glorify God in your body, and in your spirit, which are God's."*

   The nature of fire is to change the form of whatever it touches directly. We need the Holy Ghost Fire to burn out our old nature and transform us into new creatures, vessels of God's Love, Life, and Light!

4. **Fire cooks** - Acts 1:8 – *"But ye shall receive power, after that the Holy Ghost is come upon you: and ye shall be witnesses unto me both in Jerusalem, and in all Judaea, and in Samaria, and unto the uttermost part of the earth."*

> *"The Holy Ghost is a gift because we cannot do anything to earn Him."*
>
> *- Dr. John L. Godbolt*

A witness is one who leaves a record or one who is a martyr (a person who gives up his life for a cause). It means that one's life is transformed by the power of the Holy Ghost and their greatest desire is to be a living epistle and tell others about the power of the Blood of Jesus. A witness is one who no longer allows the carnal side (flesh) to rule his or her actions and behavior.

Jesus Christ was led to choose twelve men; most of whom were uneducated, poor, non-influential, and unfamiliar with this new charge of "Go ye!" over their lives. They had come to depend totally on Jesus' every word. Now, He is about to leave them. For three and a half years, Jesus changed, challenged, and comforted them through every situation and, in a matter of hours, everything was about to change. Jesus understood their helpless estate and spoke these words:

> *John 16:7 - "Nevertheless, I tell you the truth: It is expedient for you that I go away: for if I go not away, the Comforter will not come unto you; but if I depart, I will send him unto you."*

On the day of Pentecost, the Power of God exploded on the scene in the form of cloven tongues and fire (Acts 2:3). Since that time, men and women who have accepted Jesus as Savior and Lord have been filled with this life changing power. Because Jesus departed the physical and visible realms, God's Holy Spirit is able to abide in our spirit to direct, comfort, transform, consume, and conform our old nature into a new one that reflects His Image.

Notes (Summary):

Part Two:
How to Receive the Holy Ghost and Fire

Anticipation:

The Baptism of the Holy Ghost is God's Gift to You

"Then Peter said unto them. Repent, and be baptized every one of you in the name of Jesus Christ for the remission of sins, and ye shall receive the gift of the Holy Ghost. For the promise is unto you, and to your children, and to all that are afar off, even as many as the Lord our God shall call" (Acts 2:38,39).

Journaling Moment:

_____

_____

_____

_____

On the day of Pentecost, the Apostle Peter announced that the Holy Ghost was for the Jews who were present that day and that the Promise extended to their children. It also extended to those who were 'afar off' (referring to the Gentiles). Anyone who receives Jesus Christ as their personal Savior becomes a part of the family of God. Being a part of God's family makes you an heir with full rights to inherit the gift of the Holy Ghost.

> *"The Holy Ghost is the batteries in your flashlight. Your body is the flashlight, but He is the power that allows you to see the way!"*
>
> - DR. JOHN L. GODBOLT

Preparation:

Become Like a Little Child

"Whosoever therefore shall humble himself as this little child, the same is greatest in the kingdom of heaven." (Matthew 18:4).

Journaling Moment:

_____

_____

_____

_____

Jesus used metaphors, allegories, symbolism, and analogies in His teaching; therefore, He was not speaking of a literal baby or child in this text. He was speaking of persons willing to become like little children, trusting, forgetting their own birth language, and allowing the Holy Ghost to take charge of their tongues. He [the Holy Spirit] forms in us a new birth language of baby syllables until it becomes a full language, gushing out like rivers of living waters. Remember, parents influence their child's language. Likewise, the Holy Ghost is our Spiritual Parent who influences our language as we look to the Cross of Calvary and surrender our tongue to Him!

Expectation:

Expect God to Give You the Evidence of Other Tongues

"And they were all filled with the Holy Ghost, and began to speak with other tongues, as the Spirit gave them utterance" (Acts 2:4).

Journaling Moment:

_____

_____

_____

_____

Those who were waiting for the Holy Ghost began to speak with other tongues; that is, they spoke in a language that they had never learned.

God gave the miracle of tongues as a sign -- evidence that they had been baptized and filled with the Gift of the Holy Ghost. Tongues were also the sign given on the Day of Pentecost.

God never changes His method of operation.

The Word of God declares that He is the same yesterday, today and forever (Hebrews 13:8). Since God gave tongues as the sign of the Baptism of the Holy Ghost 'yesterday' -- or in Biblical days, we can be sure this is the sign He gives today.

Saturation:

Fix Your Heart and Mind on His Word

"Nevertheless I tell you the truth; it is expedient for you that I go away: for if I go not away, the Comforter will not come unto you; but if I depart, I will send him unto you" (John 16:7).

Journaling Moment:

_____

_____

_____

_____

The greatest resource in the Christian's arsenal is the Holy Bible. Learn to love it and cherish every word in it. Make it your love letter from God, our Heavenly Father, to you, His child. Think about Calvary as your greatest love story and not an event recorded in history, or even just 'your Bible'.

Jesus Christ shed His precious Blood on Calvary's Cross so that "YOU" might have a new heart created within you. This new heart grows as "YOU" focus more on prayer, repentance, and the study of the Word of God. No one can do this for you but YOU.

When in doubt, worship Him! Becoming a worshipper will set the stage for the Holy Ghost to come in and dwell within you. Begin by lifting your voice in singing, making a melody in your heart, and giving God praise for His promise of the Holy Ghost.

Before Jesus returned to His Father, He promised to send the Comforter, the blessed Holy Ghost, to us. That is why we can look steadfastly to Calvary and to the promise of this precious gift in The Word. This is how we keep our minds fixed on Jesus, who is the perfect sacrifice for our sins and the only source of cleansing of our souls.

Duration:

Patiently Wait Until You Are Empowered

"And, behold, I send the promise of my Father upon you; but tarry ye in the city of Jerusalem, until ye be endued with power from on high" (Luke 24:49).

Journaling Moment:

_____

_____

_____

_____

Jesus told His disciples to tarry. The Greek word for "tarry" is ek-dekh-om-ahee, which means to wait, to receive, to accept, to look for, and to expect. To tarry is more about your focus while you worship God. Do you see yourself receiving the Holy Spirit? Is your mind focused on Calvary, with gratitude for the crucified and risen Savior?

The disciples followed Jesus' instruction and returned to Jerusalem, where they gathered into a group of about a hundred and twenty. The scripture says that they continued in prayer and supplication until the "day of Pentecost was fully come." As they tarried on that day the Promise was fulfilled, and they were endowed (overcome) or overshadowed with the great and wonderful Power of the Holy Ghost.

Continuation:

Seek God Daily to Be Refilled

"And hope maketh not ashamed; because the love of God is shed abroad in our hearts by the Holy Ghost which is given unto us" (Romans 5:5).

Journaling Moment:

_____

_____

_____

After you have received this initial, glorious experience, be intentional to yield daily to be refilled with the power of the Holy Ghost so that your mouth will be filled continually with His Words of love.

> *"An inspired life is one ignited by the Holy Ghost!"*
>
> - Dr. John L. Godbolt

Implementation:

Use This Power to Witness

Acts 1:8 - *But ye shall receive power, after that the Holy Ghost is come upon you: and ye shall be witnesses unto me both in Jerusalem, and in all Judaea, and in Samaria, and unto the uttermost part of the earth.*

Journaling Moment:

_____

_____

_____

_____

Again, we need the Holy Ghost to work within and without. First, we need personal evidence that this power works within us to heal hidden hurts and wounds. Our daily life should illustrate that we have been changed. Secondly, we need the Holy Ghost in order to become ambassadors for Christ and to tell others about His delivering power in our personal life.

> "Even when life is difficult, the Holy Ghost comforts, strengthens and enables you to wait."
>
> - DR. JOHN L. GODBOLT

Notes (Summary):

Part Three:
Power to Wait, Witness, War and Work

The purpose of the gift of the Holy Ghost is to empower the believer to wait in God's Presence, to witness to others about His Presence, to war against other ungodly presences, and to work with the presence of mind that every work for Christ is a good work.

The biblical symbol for the Holy Ghost is the dove. He is the third person in the Godhead (Colossians 2:9). We read about Him in Genesis 1:2 when the Spirit of God *moved* upon the face of the waters. We see Him in demonstration in Genesis 8:8 when Noah sent out a dove after the Ark came to rest. We see Him in Matthew 3:16 descending upon Jesus after His baptism by John in the Jordan river. And we see Him in action on the day of Pentecost when they were all filled with the Holy Ghost and Fire and spoke with other tongues.

We can better understand the power of the Holy Ghost when we study the nature of the dove. Here are eight (8) natural characteristics of a dove and spiritual demonstration they provide:

1. **Clean** - The dove is one of the cleanest birds on earth. It will not place its feet upon anything dead, rotten, or corrupt. This is a beautiful picture of the Holy Ghost. He will not rest upon an unclean life. We must surrender to the power of the Blood and allow Jesus to cleanse areas of our life so that the Holy Ghost can enter with His power and establish residency in our will, spirit, and soul.

2. **Harmless** - Philippians 2:15 - *"That ye may be blameless and harmless, the sons of God, without rebuke, in the midst of a crooked and perverse nation, among whom ye shine as lights in the world;"* The dove does not have an aggressive

nature or dark side, but is harmless in all aspects of its life. It is the same with the gift of the Holy Ghost. Harmless means to be unmixed, pure, free from guile, simple, and innocent. When we are filled with the Holy Ghost we will have power to overcome temptations and remain pure before God and man.

3. **Gentleness** - Galatians 5:22, 23 - *"But the fruit of the Spirit is love, joy, peace, longsuffering, gentleness, goodness, faith, meekness, temperance: against such there is no law."* The dove is an extremely gentle bird by nature. It is non-threatening, even in its appearance. The Word of God defines gentleness as morally excellent in character, integrity, and kindness. When we are filled with the Holy Ghost, our old nature is transformed into a new nature like that of the dove.

4. **Faithfulness** - I Corinthians 4:2 - *"Moreover it is required in stewards, that a man be found faithful."* The dove is known for its faithfulness to one mate. If its mate dies, the remaining dove will never mate again. The Bible describes faithfulness as an outward demonstration of handling business, executing and completing commands, or the discharge of official duties. The gift of the Holy Ghost will help us in all our natural and spiritual affairs in this life. We can be faithful to our God, spouse, family, and to the call that is on our lives.

5. **Vision** - Proverbs 29:18 - *"Where there is no vision, the people perish: but he that keepeth the law, happy is he."* The dove has keen eyesight. Spiritual vision means to have dreams, revelation, and divine communication. The Holy Ghost gives us perception and the ability to contemplate the things of God, especially as they relate to our personal walk and spiritual assignment.

6. **Brooding** - Genesis 1:2 - *". . . And the Spirit of God moved upon the face of the waters."* The dove's nature is to brood over its young until they grow and develop. When it broods over its young, the dove's body hovers over the eggs to keep them warm, and its voice generates a sound that relaxes the developing eggs. The word *moved* means to brood, to be relaxed, to flutter, and to shake. When we, as believers of Jesus Christ, are covered by the Holy Ghost, we can relax and trust God to grow (mature) us up in places we are weak and lack understanding.

7. **Symbol of Peace** - Philippians 4:7 - *"And the peace of God, which passeth all understanding, shall keep your hearts and minds through Christ Jesus."* Throughout history, the emblem of the dove has been and continues to be a sign of peace. The Holy Ghost is able to rest upon us and give peace in trying times.

> *"You can lean on the Holy Ghost for revelation and explanation."*
>
> - Dr. John L. Godbolt

8. **Strength** - Psalm 55:6 - *"And I said, Oh that I had wings like a dove! For then would I fly away, and be at rest."* The dove is not known for its strength, but it is unusually powerful considering its nature and demeanor. They are fast and they have a bullet straight flight pattern. When they take off, their wings make a whistling sound. Doves have been clocked traveling at 55 mph (88.5 km/h) and they can travel 150 miles (241.4 kilometers) without resting. This feat takes incredible strength and endurance. Likewise, the Holy Ghost is an enduring power in our lives. He can speed up our prayer language, shift our thinking, give us instant

revelation (Luke 12:12), and expand our understanding of God's Word in a split second.

Notes (Summary):

> "Some things in our lives need to be cooked to perfection. Other things need to be completely burned up!"
>
> – DR. JOHN L. GODBOLT

_____

_____

_____

_____

_____

_____

_____

_____

_____

_____

_____

_____

_____

_____

_____

_____

_____

CONCLUSION

When a baby is born, all the parts for him/her to become an adult are inside and there is no need to return to the doctor for any additional parts to be added. However, it takes proper nutrients, a healthy lifestyle, rest and exercise, education, and love to ensure that the child will grow into a healthy and productive adult. This is the same premise for receiving the Holy Ghost.

When a new believer is born into the family of God through repentance of sins and accepting Jesus Christ as Savior, he/she receives a measure of the Holy Ghost but not the full stature. As natural babies grow, their need for nutrition and other ingredients increase, and it becomes essential that the necessary supplements are made available. There is no difference in regard to the gift of the Holy Ghost. The power of the Holy Ghost guides us, makes us wiser, and gives us an understanding that leads us to a higher place in Christ. To receive the full stature of the Holy Spirit, one must seek a more intimate relationship with Christ through prayer, fasting, study of the Word, brotherly fellowship, and personal worship.

I met my wife on the campus of Fayetteville State University. Both of us were born again believers and It didn't take long before we knew we had a lot in common. We fell in love and I wanted her to meet my parents. Indirectly, she had already met them because she met me. I am a product of my father and mother's love. They birth me, named me, fed me, taught me and sent me. However, it wasn't until I brought her to our home and introduced her to my parents that she had the opportunity to experience each of them. This is how our relationship with Jesus grows. John 14:6 - *Jesus saith unto him, I am the way, the truth, and the life: no man cometh unto the Father, but by me.*

Because we have accepted Jesus as our Savior and Lord, in essence, we have The Father and Holy Spirit, but not in their fullness. As with my wife, having her own private time with my parents, we need a personal experience with the Holy Spirit. Each of us must allow the indwelling power of The Holy Ghost and Fire to change us into what God intended in Genesis 1:26; *to be made in His image and likeness.*

QUOTES ON THE HOLY SPIRIT

"It is the Holy Spirit's job to convict, God's job to judge and my job to love."
Billy Graham

❧

"Will God ever ask you to do something you are not able to do? The answer is yes – all the time! It must be that way, for God's glory and kingdom. If we function according to our ability alone, we get the glory; if we function according to the power of the Spirit within us, God gets the glory. He wants to reveal Himself to a watching world."
Henry Blackaby, Experiencing the Spirit: The Power of Pentecost Every Day

❧

"In my experience, self-hatred is the dominant malaise crippling Christians and stifling their growth in the Holy Spirit."
Brennan Manning, Abba's Child: The Cry of the Heart for Intimate Belonging

❧

"The wizard (of Oz) says look inside yourself and find self. God says look inside yourself and find (the Holy Spirit). The first will get you to Kansas. The latter will get you to heaven. Take your pick."
Max Lucado, Experiencing the Heart of Jesus: Knowing His Heart, Feeling His Love

❧

"The Holy Spirit doesn't need to equip you for what you're not going to do, so if you're in rebellion against Jesus and refusing His right to be Lord, He doesn't need to send the Holy spirit to equip you for service. And, tragically, you miss out on the joy that He brings. So let the Holy Spirit deal with anything that's keeping you from obeying Christ."
Henry and Melvin Blackaby

❦

"When you strip it of everything else, Pentecost stands for power and life. That's what came into the church when the Holy Spirit came down on the day of Pentecost.
David Wilkerson, The Cross and the Switchblade

❦

"To put it simply: the Holy Spirit bothers us. Because he moves us, he makes us walk, he pushes the Church to go forward. And we are like Peter at the Transfiguration: 'Ah, how wonderful it is to be here like this, all together!'... But don't bother us. We what the Holy Spirit. And that's no good. Because he is God, he is that wind which comes and goes, and you don't know where. He is the power of God; he is the one who gives consolation and strength to move forward. But: to move forward! And this bothers us. It's so much nicer to be comfortable."
Pope Francis, Encountering Truth: Meeting God in the Everyday

❦

"The Holy Spirit will always point people to the finished work of Jesus." **John Paul Warren**

❧

"The Holy Spirit puts the 'super' into our 'natural'."
Amba Keeble

❧

"The Holy Spirit is an incredible leader and healer. Don't shove it down; lay your junk on the table and deal with it. Address the stuff. Forgive, release, acknowledge, confront, feel the feelings, let something go, believe the truth, whatever you need to do. Then dust your hands off and get ready to go."
Jen Hatmaker, *For the Love: Fighting for Grace in a World of Impossible Standards*

❧

"Clothes, coffee, books, money, achievements, perfect circumstances...none of this can come close to bringing me the joy that comes from the Holy Spirit."
Tessa Emily Hall, *Coffee Shop Devos: Daily Devotional Pick-Me-Ups for Teen Girls*

❧

"When we learn how to battle with the sword of the Spirit, with its two edges of the Word and God's Holy Spirit, the enemy will flee before us."
Linda Evans Shepherd, *Winning Your Daily Spiritual Battles*

❧

"The Bible distinguishes between 'having' the Holy Spirit, which is true of all believers, and being 'filled' with the Holy Spirit, which is true of very few."
Oswald J. Smith, *The Enduement of Power: Being Filled with The Holy Spirit*

❦

"The Holy Spirit is no sceptic, and the things He has written in our hearts are not doubts or opinions, but assertions – surer and more certain than sense and life itself."
Martin Luther, *The Bondage of the Will*

❦

"Your body is a temple of the Holy Spirit."
Lailah Gifty Akita

❦

"The Holy Spirit will teach you how to distinguish between right and wrong doctrines."
Sunday Adelaja

Our Thoughts

The gift of the Holy Ghost is the supernatural power of God for witnessing about Christ (Acts 1:8), for enjoying a deeper and more intimate relationship with Jesus, and for living a victorious Christian life.

The baptism of the Holy Ghost is a gift to everyone who has accepted Jesus Christ as their Savior and Lord over his or her life. This book is a step-by-step teaching tool with space for journaling to encourage the reader to believe in this gift and to receive it as the Holy Bible promises.

John L. Godbolt is the CEO of ReDeemed Christian Churches International Inc. and Partners in Marriage (PiM) Inc. He is an educator, mentor, life coach, and conference speaker. He has been married to Vertell since 1973. They have two married children and six grandchildren.

www.partnersinmarriage.com

Photo by: Reginald Ennett of One Flesh Photography